Descriptive Account of the Island of Trinidad, 1797

F Mallet

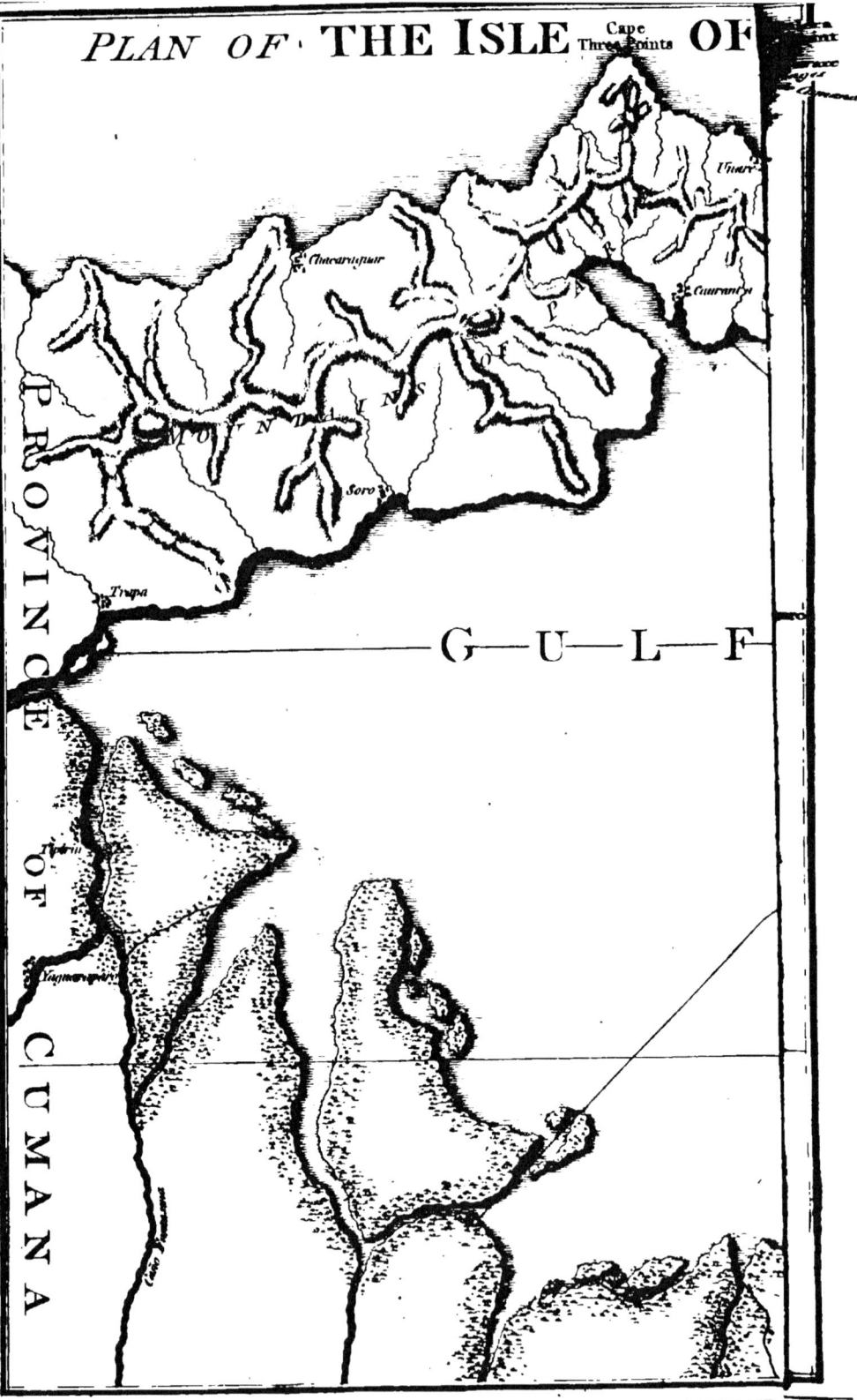

PLAN OF THE ISLE OF

Cape
Three Points

Chacarapar

Uraré

St. Caurant?

P

Soro

M O U N T A I N S

Trapa

P R O V I N C E   O F   C U M A N A

G U L F

Vidrin

Yaqueraquen

DESCRIPTIVE ACCOUNT

OF THE

ISLAND OF TRINIDAD:

MADE BY ORDER OF

SIR RALPH ABERCROMBIE, K. B.

LIEUTENANT-GENERAL AND COMMANDER IN CHIEF OF THE BRITISH FORCES IN THE WEST INDIES;

BY F. MALLET, CAPT. OF THE SURVEYING ENGINEERS,

1797.

INSULA DIVES OPUM.   VIRGIL.

PRINTED ON FOUR SHEETS OF LARGE ATLAS PAPER:

*In which are delineated all the Lands granted by the
Crown of Spain since the first Establishment; likewise
all those Lands which remain to be granted, and are
suitable for various Manufactures and Plantations; dis-
tinguishing also the Mountains, Rivers, Savana and Marsh
Lands; Royal Roads, Indian Paths, Anchoring Places,
Rocks, Sand-Banks, &c. with the Soundings round the
Island in Fathoms.*

ACCOMPANIED WITH A GENERAL CHART OF THE GULPH OF PARIA.

LONDON:

PRINTED FOR

W. FADEN, GEOGRAPHER TO THE KING, AND TO

HIS ROYAL HIGHNESS THE PRINCE OF WALES,

CHARING CROSS.

Price One Pound Seven Shillings the MAP and DESCRIPTION.

Smerton, St. Martin's Lane.

1802.

THE

ISLAND

OF

TRINIDAD

LIES on the North-Eaſt Coaſt of South America, near the entrance of the River Orinoco (Oroonoko) in the 11° of north Latitude, and 61° Longitude Weſt of London. It is the largeſt and ſouthernmoſt of all the Leeward Iſlands, meaſuring in its extreme length from Eaſt to Weſt 60 Britiſh miles, and from North to South 45 miles; containing 2,400 ſquare miles ſuperficial meaſure. It muſt be obſerved here, as one of the peculiar advantages of this Iſland, that it is without the reach of the Hurricanes ſo deſtructive in Jamaica and ſome other Iſlands. Trinidad was diſcovered by Chriſtopher Columbus, in his third voyage, July 31ſt, 1498, and ſo named from its appearance, at 13 leagues diſtance to the S. E. with three heads or mountains above all the reſt. It was then inhabited by Caribs of a very mild diſpoſition, induſtrious, well made, and of a whiter colour than that of the people of the other iſlands. The greateſt part of them however were already deſtroyed, in 1518, when the Spaniards, for working the mines, made ſlaves of all the Indians they could kidnap, under the abominable pretence that they were man-eaters: The virtuous *las Casas* could reſcue but very few inhabitants of Trinidad from this general Proſcription.

Sir *Walter Raleigh*, who was in the Iſland of Trinidad in 1593, remarks upon it as being very proper for the cultivation of Tobacco and Sweet Canes; alſo of the Spaniards having told him, that Gold could be found in the Iſland, chiefly in the beds of the rivers.

The Spaniſh accounts of Trinidad are very few, and remarkably deficient; Father *Joſeph Gumilla*, from whom we might have expected a complete deſcription of the Iſland, has taken very little notice of it in his Hiſtory of the Oroonoko *(Orinoco illuſtrado).*

B

Abbé

Abbé Raynal, in the *Histoire politique et philosophique des deux Indes*, says, " the defign of the firft fettlement of this Ifland was for the purpofe of fecuring the conqueft of the Orinoco."

Alcedo, in his *Dictionary of the Weft Indies and America*, is the only Spanifh Author who has entered into fome detail concerning Trinidad; he fpeaks with rapture of its fertility, its numerous and various productions; fuch as excellent Grapes, an innumerable quantity of Oranges of the moft exquifite flavour; of Seville Oranges, Citrons, Lemons, &c. befides all the fruits peculiar to the Weft Indies. It produces likewife Coffee, and fupplies the Ifland of Margarita and feveral other places with Mayze. The article of Indigo is particularly noticed as growing wild in great abundance of the beft quality, and the Cocoa as being equally good with that of the Province of Caracoa, which is efteemed the beft of the Spanifh Weft-Indies; Gumilla fays, that it was preferred by the Traders to the Cocoa of the Caraccas; but that the plantations, or Cocoa walks, have been fo neglected fince the year 1727, that there are fcarce any left now in the ifland; in fhort, thefe productions are fuch, that the Difcoverers, comparing it with the other Iflands, diftinguifhed it by the name of The PARADISE.

The Map of the Ifland of Trinidad, which this brief account is intended to accompany, appears to have been grounded on the Spanifh Maritime Survey made by order of Government in 1793, and the Topography of the Interior to have been executed by Mr. Mallet in 1797, under the directions of the late Sir Ralph Abercrombie, K. B. when the Britifh Forces took poffeffion of the Ifland. In the prefent Map all the Plots of Land which have been granted by the Crown of Spain fince its firft Eftablifhment are carefully laid down, divided into Quarters, diftinguifhing thofe which have Settlements, together with the Proprietors Names, of whom a Lift is annexed. The Map likewife exhibits all thofe Lands remaining to be difpofed of, which are laid out in Lots (numbered) containing 100 Squares, or 320 Acres; each Square being 100 Paces of 3¼ feet long, is equal to 3¼ Acres.——The Lots are divided into Quarters or Diftricts, for the purpofe of afcertaining their refpective Situations, and other local advantages; thefe Lands are in general covered with very thick Woods.

In this Ifland there are three diftinct *Ridges of Mountains*, the *Northern*, *Middle* and *Southern*, which are moftly inacceffible, and covered with all kinds of incorruptible Woods proper for Ship-Building*.

---

* The Ifland, fays *Alcedo*, is a continual Foreft of precious Timber, fuch as Cedars, Walnut-trees of feveral forts; Palm Trees of various Kinds, Guayacum Tree," &c.

The

The *Rivers*, feveral of which are confiderable, have been traced and examined as to what diftance they are navigable, and alfo with refpect to the improvements they may be capable of by deepening their Beds, new Canals, &c.

The navigable Rivers on the Weft Coaft or Gulph, are the Caroni, Guaracara, Coura, and Siparia; thofe on the Eaft Coaft are the Ortoire, Neg, Lebranche, and the Oropuche, all which abound with many kinds of Fifh; but thofe on the Eaft Coaft are particularly frequented by Sharks; by the Lamentin (Sea Cow or Manattee) weighing generally from 500 to 800 cwt. fometimes 16 cwt. it is harpooned like the whale, and its flefh is very good frefh or dry: fome of this fpecies have been caught in the French Antilles, meafuring 20 feet in length and 10 in breadth; you meet alfo with the *Pantouflier*, or *Zigene*, a dangerous and voracious monfter, about 10 or 12 feet long, and thick in proportion; its head is fhaped like a hammer, having large round terrific eyes, a wide mouth well armed with teeth, and more conveniently difpofed for biting than thofe of the Shark, whofe body it moft refembles. This Fifh is common in the French Antilles, and hath been often found at Guadalupe, in the Road of Baffe Terre.

The *Caroni* is the principal River of the Ifland, being navigable from its entrance in the Gulph of Paria to the Aripo, a diftance of nearly 20 Britifh miles.

The *Aripo*, a branch of the Caroni, is navigable; which, by means of a Canal to connect it with the Guaro, (a branch of the Oropuche alfo navigable to the Sea); a communication might be opened from the Weft Coaft or Gulph of Paria to the Eaft Coaft or Atlantic.

The *Guanape*, or *Guanaba*, a branch of the Caroni, is alfo navigable, but hath lefs depth of water than the Aripo.

Coura River, on the Weft Coaft is capable of being made navigable to the diftance of 5,000 paces.

The *River Siparia* is navigable to the diftance of 3,000 paces, and might be extended to 7,000.

The *Ortoire* or *Guataro*, is the principal River on the Eaft Coaft, having from its entrance to the Morne Orange (a diftance of about 20 miles) two, four, and five fathoms; but the mouth of this River being fhoal water, it would be requifite to cut a navigable Canal of 2,600 paces from the Ortoire (between the Settlements of Guias and Thomazo) to the Bay of Mayaro, thereby giving the utmoft facility of exportation to the productions of this immenfe tract of cultivable Land. The Anchorage in Mayaro Bay is fafe, having good holding ground with a bottom of fand and

gravel.

gravel. You may embark or difembark in this Bay at any time of the Tide. The Tide is perceivable in this River about the junction of the Moura.

The *Neg* or *Nariva River* runs parallel to the fhore at a fhort diftance from it, forming a Canal of about five or fix miles in length, with three, four, and five fathoms; it receives the Waters of the Mangrove Trees, which fpread over all this part. The water of this River is black, and fo much tainted as to render the Sea frothy throughout the Bay. There are two navigable Channels, connecting the Rivers Neg and Ortoire, which greatly facilitate the draining of thofe Rivers when inundated.

Lebranche, this River is navigable to the diftance of 6,000 paces, the Marfhes at the entrance might be drained with facility.

The *River Oropuche* is navigable to the uppermoft branch, called the Guaro (a length of 18 miles) from which a Canal might be made to the Aripo, and thereby connect the two oppofite Streams of the Oropuche and Caroni.

Savanas, of which there are feveral in this Ifland. Savana Grande, or Great Savana of Caroni, is a large tract of drowned Land, part in Savana, although flooded in the rainy feafons. Notwithftanding the center of this Marfh is level with the Sea, yet a confiderable portion of it might be fuccefsfully drained by making ftrait Cuts to connect the inflections of the River Caroni; the narrow Channels of which from becoming incumbered at the the time of the inundations, overflow all the Lands adjoining thereto.

The *Laguna Grande*, or the Great Lagoon, is another tract of Marfh Land, inacceffible.—Thefe Savanas produce a great quantity of the Mangrove trees.

Marfh of Icaque, in this Savana, which is level with the Sea, are two Gulfs; one of which hath an elevation of feven feet, the other thirteen; mud and calcareous earth are continually gufhing out of them. Two of the principal Mouths produce detonations in the months of March and June, throwing up at the fame time metallic particles, ftones rounded by friction, and other heterogeneous fubftances.

The other Marfhes are thofe of Ortoire, Oropuche, and the Mangroves.

At *Cape de la Brea* (the weftern extremity of the Great Lagoon) is a Lake of Bitumen or Pitch, fituated 80 feet above the level of the Sea, and very extenfive; good water may always be found in fome of the openings at two, four, and eight feet depth; there are alfo fome fmall Iflands of the Mangrove trees. The fort of Pitch which is beft for the ufe of Shipping, is found in the center of the Lake; upon any pieces of it being cut out

with

with an axe or otherwife, the chafms will fill up immediately.—The
feveral branches of this Lake are level throughout, extending towards the
Sea, but are all fuftained by the main Spring or focus. The Village of
la Brea is eftablifhed upon one of thefe Branches, but the Pitch that is
found near the Sea has received more heat, and contains a greater quantity
of heterogeneous fubftances. Father Gumilla tells us, that about 60 years
ago, a little before he came to Trinidad, a fpot of land on the Weftern
Coaft, near half way between the Capital and the Indian Village, did fink
fuddenly, and was immediately replaced by a fmall lake of Pitch to the
great furprife and terror of the inhabitants.

The *Weftern Coaft* of the Ifle of Trinidad, with the oppofite Coaft of
the Province of Cumana, form the extenfive Gulph of Paria, named by
Columbus, Golfo de Ballena, or Gulph of the Whale. There is good
Anchorage in this Gulf on the Coaft of Trinidad, having from 3 to 10 and
16 fathoms water, mud bottom.

Chaguaramas Harbour lies on the north Shore of this Gulph, about
three leagues weft of Port of Spain; is capable of receiving the largeft
Ships of War, having from 4 to 25 and 40 fathoms water, gravel and ooze
bottom; the Shores are bold and fteep. When the Britifh Forces attacked
the Ifland in 1797, the Spaniards burnt in this Harbour one Ship of 80
guns, two of 74 guns, and one Frigate of 32 guns.

The *Careening Place* (le Carenage) is fhallow, having from two to
four fathoms water, and therefore is fuitable for Merchant Ships only.

Gafpar Grande,—on this Ifland the Spaniards have conftructed a
Battery of Mafonry to protect the Harbour; it is ill fituated, and without
folidity.

Port of Spain (Puerto d'Efpana) is fituated on the North-Eaft Coaft
of the Gulf of Paria, having a Jetty or Quay of Mafonry, with a Battery
en Barbette even with the water's edge for the defence of the Town; here
are alfo two other Batteries on the eaft fide.

The Bay before this port is one of the fafeft and moft extenfive in the
world; fhips being able to anchor there in a fuperficial fpace of above 70
miles, with a depth of Water from 12 to five fathoms only one mile off
fhore, and all good holding ground. Should they drive from their anchors,
they go on fhore in foft mud, and are got off without damage. A white
half-moon Battery, juft above the town, on the brow of the hill, is a good
Mark for the Bay, and may be feen a long way off: This Battery, by
large fhips, fhould never be brought to the northward of N. N. E. and the
beft anchorage is in the north-weft bight of the Bay.

Sᴛ.

St. Joseph de Oruna, the capital Town of the Island, is situated seven miles east from the Port of Spain; on the road between these two places, is the Village St. John.

Indian Missions in this Island, among the few Caribs which remain of its first inhabitants, are those of *Arima, Toco, Gayaro, Cumana, Monserat, Savana Grande,* and *Siparia*.

The *Population* of Trinidad, according to the account taken in July, 1797 (see the annexed Table) amounted to seventeen thousand, seven hundred and eighteen souls, including all descriptions.

Near *Cape la Brea*, a little to the south-west, is a Gulph or Vortex in the Sea, which, in stormy weather, gushes out, raising the water five or six feet, and covers the surface for a considerable space with Panoleum or Tar.

On the *East Coast* in the *Bay of Mayaro*, there is another Gulf or Vortex, similar to the former, which, in the months of March and June, produces a detonation like thunder, having some flame with a thick black smoke which vanishes away immediately; in about 24 hours afterwards is found along shore of the Bay, a quantity of Bitumen or Pitch, about three or four inches thick, which is employed with success.

Along the Shore of *Cocos Bay* to the distance of about 50 paces, are found a great quantity of Palm or Cocoa Trees, whose species is not natural to the Island; a Launch coming from the River Orinoco, laden with Cocoa Nuts, was wrecked in this Bay, by which accident these trees were planted and continue to multiply.

We shall conclude this short, but perhaps comprehensive account, considering the scantiness of our materials, with some observations on the Gulph of Paria, and the Lands which surround it; and on the River Orinoco, a great part of whose Waters are discharged in that Gulf.

The Gulph of Paria, received at first the several names of *Gulf of the Whale, Gulph Triste,* and *Fresh Water Sea*; its length from East to West is about 30 sea leagues, and its breadth from North to South about 15: The lesser arm of Rio Orinoco, named *Cano de Pedernales* ("channel of the Pebbles") and an immense number of smaller branches of various widths, all flowing in a northerly direction from the main Stream of the Orinoco, bring the tribute of their Waters to this inland Sea. It has two great issues into the Atlantic Ocean; namely, the Northern Mouth divided into four openings, three small ones on the eastern side, and a large one about two leagues broad on the west part, adjoining to Paria the Continent. To this Columbus gave the name of the *Dragon's Mouth*, as he had given that of the *Serpent's Mouth*, to the eastern issue of the Gulph in the Atlantic, which

which is about three leagues broad, with a fmall Ifland (called Soldiers Ifland) belonging to Trinidad in the middle of it.

On the North fide the Gulf is feparated from the Atlantic Sea by a narrow neck of fertile Land, which Columbus has named *Paria*, it is occupied by a few Indians, whofe villages, chiefly along the Coaft, are thinly fcattered; the Spaniards had lately in that part fome fettlements of French Emigrants from the Antilles; but according to report thefe Colonifts have been lately expelled.

The weft and fouth fides of the Gulph are all low, fwampy grounds, but efpecially the fouth fide as far as the Cano de Pedernales, where the Orinoco might be faid to begin, and which is the Canal of communication with the main Stream of the River; the length of this Channel is about 50 leagues, and its navigation not difficult.

All the part belonging to the River is remarkable for its periodical overflowings; the Orinoco begining to fwell in April, increafes progreffively during five months, and rifes on the fixth to its greateft height. In October it begins to decreafe gradually till the month of March, during the whole of which it is at the loweft level of its diminution. Thefe alternate variations are regular and even invariable.

This Phenomenon, the caufe of which is unknown, appears according to *Abbé Raynal*, to depend more on the Sea than on the Land: during the five months of the River's increafe, the hemifphere of the new World, in fome degree expofes only Seas, and fcarce any Lands to the perpendicular action of the folar rays: during the following fix months of the River's decreafe, the immenfe Continent of America only is prefented to that fame action; the Sea then is lefs fubject to the active influence of the fun, or at leaft its fhelving towards the eaftern Coaft is counterbalanced, and broken in a ftronger degree by the Lands; it muft therefore leave a greater freedom to the courfe of the Rivers, which being in that cafe not fo clofely kept back by the Sea, can be fwelled only by the melting of the Snow in the fouthern Cordilleras, or by the rains. Perhaps alfo it is the rainy feafon which determines the increafe of the Orinoco; we fhall add that this is the opinion of Father Gumilla, who feems to have examined this fingular effect with great attention. "When fome enlightened nation, concludes "Abbé Raynal, fhall become acquainted with the banks of the Orinoco, "the phenomena of its courfe will be known, or at leaft they will be "thoroughly ftudied."

The branches of the Orinoco, as numerous as they are intricate, form a multitude of Iflands of different fizes, which you find covered with palm trees; although their foil lies under water during fix months of the year, and

the

the tide covers it twice a day ; they are inhabited by the *Guaraunos*, who have found the means of constructing commodious huts on high piles deeply driven in the mud, and sometimes to build them in the trees themselves, which at the same time supply them with food, drink, household furniture, canoes, &c. &c. These Indians are supposed to be about six thousand, their language is soft, easily learnt, and spoken by all the Spanish traders of Gayana ; they are very expert fishermen, and trade in fish, nets, baskets, &c. made with the leaves of their palm trees. They are a mild, gay and sociable nation, always dancing, and at peace with every body.

F I N I S.

J. Smeeton, Printer, 148, St. Martin's Lane, Westminster.

LIST

OF

PROPRIETORS OF LAND

IN THE

ISLAND OF TRINIDAD,

MARCH 20th, 1797.

V. Benfils	}	
Mandillon		
Le Fevre		
Belgent	} Point a Piérre	
V. Pechier		
Letain		
D'Vineta	}	
V. Pechier	}	
Loreille		
Rochard		
Mongonge		
Salvador		
Dubois		
Vincent		
Pilatre		
Picou		
Blondel	} Naparima	
Juillet		
Bontour		
Caille		
Clairmen		
Bordénave		
Treit		
Deravine		
Clarck	}	

Nugent	}	
Bernard		
Sipriani		
Renau		
Borde		
Bouler		
Gracien		
Rambert		
Oliver		
Sr. Martin		
Francique		
D'Coll		
Serrat	} Naparima	
Anfries		
Cupet		
Sardien		
Crivel		
Thelor		
Hudes		
Langtan		
Morin		
Godinee		
Polesias		
Fifague		
Pradon		
Letrain	}	

Trabau		Allatre	
Polerie		Duchatel	
Oroser	} Siparia	Huet	
Voisin		Mer. Huet	
Toulisier		Mahan	
Hilaire		Hugues	
		Duitron	
Vatable		Juan Radin	
Boucuu		Selier	
Durigne		De Burel	
Boye		Ruanet	
Oditto		Suranpar	} Mayaro
Dandon		Cardoniere	
Vancc		Dupuch	
Cadue		Fronlin	
Dubois	} Brea	h'Lahai	
Dance		Ipolite	
Gougon		Romain	
Deprace		Desten	
Coander		Redou	
Lesier		Rose	
Papin		Raphad	
Fortin			
		Pedre	
La Mote		Guide	
Long		Rose	
L'Patiance	} Trois	Louis	
Honoré		P. Martin	
Marsiany		Lignes	
Qorge		Martao	
		Robert	
Capeville	Icaque	Lignes	} Guayaguayare
		Fontin	
Lesade	Erin	Blans	
		Palanquin	
Radia		Rigo	
Guias	} Mayaro	Copstus	
Thomaso		Rigo	
Mahan		Durefor	

S. Martin		Rolan	
Desqueruche		Roche	
Me. Robert		Du Couron	
Bisaque		Dominique	
Guide		Begeré	
Tenebre		Olivier	
Balan	Guayaguayare	Sorre	
Rogie		Labarene	
Ruanel		Dufally	
Bernard		Teansie	
Moncreau		Semian	Diego Martin
Godin		Moro	
Gilulau		Felicite	
		Audiber	
Sippiuni		Gealtroi	
Mercie		Audiber	
Traiton		Pouchet	
Elic		Desoon	
Dert		Portel	
Bodin		Julien	
D'guspar		Gros	
Percin			
Joyen			
Nicol	Carénage	Mendez	
Noel		Winderflet	
Simon		Chapel	
Gardin		Pecennin	
Betteran		Devuach	Maraval
Rochard		Lotom	
Duvivur		Ludeves	
Ozelet		Gousales	
Dumas		Pechier	
Gélino			
		Dert	
Minget		Danglade	
Petieté		Fayelle	
Sicar	Diego Martin	Huet	Tagarette
Duran		Bignon	
Audier		Vignon	

Roblos		Creny	
Jermin		Lynch	
Farfan		Farfan	
Mosquire		Gaspar	
Lesaine		Legendre	St. Joseph
Gama		Purtel	
Tourn	Maracas	Magnemar	
Rivain		Lufay	
Guérino			
Gene		Geugnon	
Miver		Solger	
Aralby		S. Pern	
		Dauson	Tacarigua
Porlet		Joseph	
Black		Obrien	
Sousane		Robinson	
Charbon		Mucarti	
Nugent			
Clark	Sta. Cruz	Chaumet	Arouca
Courville		Teblau	
Martin			
Farfan		Narcise	
Cosle		Jacquis	
Laforet		Traille	
		Guiro	
Morel		D'Godet	
Norare		Ponne	Cumana or Toco
Felix		Guiro	
Farfas		Dupi	
Cazenove		Monique	
Lapargan		Rotan	
Ulorte			
Gardien	St. Joseph	Mulispine	
Indare		S. Aurin	Quiaouane
Miane		Purre	
Cajeton			
Novari		Pilard	
Topez		Diguine	Casahal
Silier		Ramsay	

Henitson		Favel	
Iguius		Samerson	
Nugent	Casahal	Duchaleau	
Waldrop		Aluson	
Warner		Farfan	Savaneta
Robertson		V. Safon	
		Cofine	
Dyckson		General Cuyler,	
Codet	Savaneta	Commander in Chief,	
Jantis		1920 Acres.	

| Names of Quarters | INDIANS. | | | |
	Women.	Boys.	Girls.	Total.
Las Bocas - - - -	—	—	—	213
Le Carenage - - -	—	—	—	802
Diego Martin - - -	—	—	—	1154
Mucurapa - - - -	—	—	—	309
Tragarette - - - -	—	—	—	276
St. Anne - - - -	—	—	—	644
Maraval - - - - -	—	—	—	611
Santa Cruz - - - -	—	—	—	374
La Ventille - - - -	—	—	—	419
Simaronero - - - -	—	—	—	323
Arieagua - - - -	—	—	—	589
ST. JOSEPH - - - -	—	—	—	728
Maracal - - - - -	—	—	—	248
Las Coiras - - - -	—	—	—	64
Tacarigua and Arouca	—	—	—	802
Arima and Guanapo -	184	105	96	717
Toco, Salibia, and Cuma	50	20	28	399
Mayaro - - - - -	—	—	—	401
Guayaguayare - - -	—	—	—	410
Erin - - - - -	—	—	—	79
Icaque and Gallos - -	—	—	—	375
La Brea - - - - -	—	—	—	555
Siparia - - - - -	49	26	14	140
Naparima - - - -	—	—	—	1379
Monserrat & Savana Gran	118	39	48	293
Pointe a Pierre - - -	—	—	—	292
Savanetta, Cuba & Casca	—	—	—	617
Puerto d'España - -	—	—	—	4525
Total -	401	190	186	17718

Abstract of the Account.

	Whites.	Colour.	Slaves.	Indians.	Total.
Men -	994	1196	4164	305	6659
Women -	590	1624	3505	401	6120
Boys -	301	898	1232	190	2621
Girls -	266	758	1108	186	2318
Total -	2151	4476	10009	1082	17718

SERVATIONS.

Tacarigua	- -	V Coffee and Cocoa only.
Arouca	- -	D flat Land, and communicates with the River Caroni.
Aripo	- -	Rnade into Sugar Plantations, from the facility of cutting Canals.
Guaro	- -	Rving a light Soil, it may be extended into the Vallies of the Northern Mountains.
Caroni	- -	Nd, and Navigable Canals made through it.
Guiaouana	-	S
Belle plaine	-	
Tamana	-	M nearly the whole of these Quarters are suitable for the Culture of Sugar Canes.
Muro	- -	R
Monferrat	- -	Mre in Ridges, near each other; fit for Coffee.
Savana Grande	-	ept Cotton.
Orange	-	M Ortoire, and is not very hilly ; these three Districts may be enlarged.
Moura	-	Rver Ortoire; the Soil is good and well drained.
Le Grand Fond	-	nt of the Navigation of the Ortoire.
Carape	- -	Pr all forts of Plantations.
Cascajal	- -	P
Savanetta	-	A
Punta de Piedras	-	P
Naparima	-	N of the Colony ; hath two navigable Rivers.
Siparia	- -	Mior of the Land is fandy, having a white Sand to the depth of three Feet, and red
La Brea	-	Pgar and Coffee.
Guapo	-	Bfuperior Quality for the Culture of Sugar Canes and Coffee.
Cedro et Irois	-	Bhe Interior ; it is fit for Sugar and Coffee only.
Quemada	-	Be Neighbourhood of Icaque is damp and marfhy.
Erin	- -	Eaccount of the eafy Communication with both Coafts.
Chagonaray	-	Fevery Sort of Culture.
Curao	- -	F is capable of being enlarged.
Morruga	-	Fiency of the Landing Places, is fit for every kind of Culture.
Guayaguayare	-	F and Coffee only.
Mayaro	- -	Rank of the Ortoire, but on approaching to Guayaguay, the Cultivation becomes more
Ortoire	- -	Fhigh ; a Canal might be made, which would communicate with Mayaro.
Cocos	- -	El hath a fruitful Soil.
L'Ebranche	-	Embarcadaire, or Landing Place, at his Entrance, and another at the Point Mancenille.
Oropuche	-	avigable Canal, to open a Communication between the Rivers Oropuche and Caroni.
Matura	-	E, and the low Lands for Cocoa ; the Soil is very productive.
Balandra	-	F and rugged ; it has two Embarcadaires, or Landing Places, and communicates with
Cumana	-	Is the East Coast only.
Grand Riviere	-	ight be established in this Quarter, the Soil being very good, but has little depth.

Coaft, are covered with all kinds of incorruptible Wood, fit for Ship Building ; the
garay, Erino, Quemada, Cedro, Irois, Guapo, la Brea and Naparina, abound in
apa Wood.

LaVergne, TN USA
08 March 2011
219313LV00004B/105/P